In Sickness and In Health

God's Continuous Miracles

JAMES NUTT

KP PUBLISHING COMPANY

ISBN: 979-8-9857-1844-7 (Paperback)
ISBN: 979-8-9857-1845-4 (Ebook)
Library of Congress Control Number: 2022906789

Editor: Renee Aldrich
Cover Design: Juan Roberts
Interior Design: Jennifer Houle
Literary Director: Sandra Slayton James

Published by:

KP Publishing Company
Publisher of Fiction, Nonfiction & Children's Books
Valencia, CA 91355
www.kp-pub.com

Printed in the United States of America

DEDICATION

This book is dedicated to my beautiful wife and best friend, Cheryl Nutt, who has stuck by my side for over thirty-nine years during times that were often difficult. Nobody will truly know the things she's had to endure. She never complained and has made many sacrifices for me and our family. You are truly a strong woman of God who was created just for me. Thank you for not giving up on me and for putting up with me even when I wasn't the best patient. Thank you for loving me unconditionally and for honoring our wedding vows, "In Sickness and in Health." Words could not express my love for you.

ACKNOWLEDGMENTS

I would like to thank my family and friends for always being there for me and for never giving up on me even when I wanted to. I now realize that if it hadn't been for your prayers, love, and support, I would have given up a long time ago. I am truly thankful and blessed to have all of you in my life. I would also like to give a special shout-out to my physician and friend for over 39 years, Dr. Harold Baer, who has been there for me since day one. Thank you for always putting forth your best effort to find the problem and the solution even when it was most difficult. You are truly a doctor sent by God just for me.

CONTENTS

INTRODUCTION

My book describes the tears, fears, challenges, and accomplishments of living with Systemic Lupus and Chronic Kidney Disease. While reading my book, you will see how hard I've had to fight just to stay alive for more than 39 years. I will also show you how this dreadful disease has not only affected my mind, body, soul, and spirit, but my family as well. The intent of my story is to inspire, uplift, and encourage especially those who may be going through similar experiences. I am a living witness that with God on your side, you can make it.

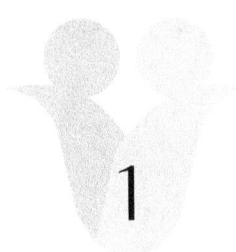

1

In the Beginning

In 1981, I was only 20 years old; I had two jobs, one working for a bank and another helping my dad with his janitorial business. I had a beautiful two-year-old daughter, Caprisha La'Shay, born on October 24, 1979. My life had essentially just begun. I had many dreams and aspirations for my future. One moment I was pretty much enjoying my life, and the next, I was trying to figure out where my health issues were coming from.

I had been an athlete in high school and college. My basketball skills shined and were well represented in my numbers; it is safe to say I was feeling pretty good about who I was as a young man and what my future held. I came from a middle-class family, a two-parent household; my father was a hardworking man, and I always knew him to work two jobs. He passed that work ethic down to me and I was on track for a great life. Then the first encounter with the sickness occurred, which would hold me hostage and send me on all kinds of ups and downs and challenge my family for more than 40 years.

It started innocently enough, like a common cold—with a cough and fever. But this common cold turned out to be not quite so common. It would evolve into excruciating chest pain. The irony of this was that I was one of those people who rarely felt bad or ever got sick. Somehow, I managed to get up and go to work with my dad anyway. As time went on it became a huge struggle for me, and I finally went to my dad and told

1

him how badly I was feeling and that I couldn't finish my workday with him. I was also unable to go to work at the bank that day. He took me home, and I felt so awful about not finishing my work with him because I knew how he depended on me, but he understood and knew something was definitely wrong with me. While at home, I tried to get some sleep thinking maybe I was just worn out, but as I tried lying down, I found the pain to increase even more in my chest area. I then decided to try sleeping while sitting up, which gave me some relief but not enough. I starred at the ceiling and wondered what was happening with my body. I was finally able to doze off when suddenly my bedroom door opened. Both my parents walked in to see how I was feeling. I told them that my condition had not improved and I was still in a lot of pain. My parents decided to take me to the emergency room to find out what was going on.

The initial report was not good; I was informed by the doctor that I had fluid around my lungs that would have to be drained. The doctors were still trying to figure out what was going on—after a few days, I was diagnosed with Pericarditis, which is a swelling and irritation of a sack like membrane surrounding the heart (pericardium). Finally, the diagnosis came that would spiral my body, mind, and spirit downward. Systemic Lupus; Systemic Lupus Erythematous (SLE) is an autoimmune disease in which the body's immune system mistakenly attacks healthy tissue. It can affect the skin, joints, kidneys, brain, and other organs. Here I was, a young man of 20! I was just beginning my life and told that I'd have to start fighting for my life, and that fight would go on far beyond 15 rounds.

I had never heard of Lupus before, I didn't know what it meant or how debilitating it was; as I looked around, I could not figure it out. Of course, I questioned over and over again, "why me?" I was too young to consider that this was the way of life and "why not me." I considered my background; I grew up in Bakersfield, California. My mother and father had five children, of which I was the second to the oldest and the only son.

As I previously mentioned, I was an athlete and had always been fit. I broke records early in my basketball days in high school, and I currently still hold the record today for having an average of 80% of free-throws in basketball. So contracting this illness made no logical sense to me; it was challenging to accept. Plus, it didn't help that I had a two-year-old daughter that I needed to take care of. My high school sweetheart, Cheryl, and I found out the news of our child just before we graduated. When we were 12 years old in junior high school, we met and started dating our junior year. We were very close and loved each other very much, so other than struggling to tell our parents; we were not opposed to having a family even though we were very young.

Our togetherness made perfect sense to us. Before we got married, we weren't always together and often went separate ways. Although we had our issues before we got married, we always reconnected and couldn't stay away from each other for too long. We always had a special bond that nobody could ever come between us. We were both enrolled in Bakersfield College but ultimately decided to step away from school to get jobs so we could take care of our child. I was able to get a job at a savings and loan bank and continued working with my dad in his janitorial business. Cheryl began working for Kern County; it would be her job until retirement.

So nothing in my life lent itself to learning that I had these kinds of health issues. Initially, I tried to keep working—this was very important to me. But it wasn't to be; I was often in and out of the hospital, and one time while at the bank, I got very weak and light-headed and passed out, and an ambulance was called for me. I knew then my job at the bank would be over. Along with more subsequent hospital visits, I was finally put on total disability, throwing me into a complete depression. Total disability at the age of 21, with my whole life ahead of me, was completely incomprehensible. But the doctor gave me what would be a lifesaving suggestion—it was in this suggestion where God first began to show up with the drops of miracles he placed along our pathway over the years. My doctor suggested I take up a hobby since I was on permanent disability.

It was then that I started experimenting with wood as a hobby. This hobby would turn into a love for the craft and an amazing skill—a God-given gift that would go a long way in creating a fluid income for us—One that would really come in handy for our family. I started working in my parent's garage, making the smaller things (plant hangers, name plates and wall clocks) to larger, more complicated items like kitchen cabinets, wall units, and bedroom sets. My clientele began to grow just by word-of-mouth. As time went by, I advanced to building larger items, such as custom closets, whenever the disease permitted. This craft not only kept me busy, but it also kept my mind off of the disease, and it became my therapy. It also gave me something to look forward to throughout the day. I guess you could say it was an escape for me and the disease. I found it very ironic that as I became stricken and robbed of my abilities as I knew them, God took that brokenness and turned me into a master craftsman.

This new skill would prove invaluable to me in many ways—it would become one of the ways I remained able to take care of my family. But it also gave me something to look forward to throughout the day. Most of all, it provided an opportunity for me to give back. I was able to give back by mentoring young men who were also interested in the craft. Many times I would allow them to help me when needed. My goal was to keep them off the streets and out of trouble.—Thus giving me another layer of satisfaction.

In building the furniture, I found peace, and it was my time alone with God as well. Yes, I was very angry, hurt, and confused, and was constantly asking myself and God, "Why Me?" Finally, I had to realize it wasn't God doing this to me, and I had to stop blaming him. I still, until this day, don't know why me, but I do know there is a reason for everything. I now have so many testimonies and situations that nobody but God has been able to bring me through. My faith and trust in God have definitely grown throughout the years! God would show me so much more as time went on.

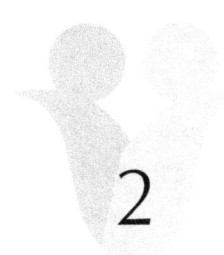

2

Married In the Midst of My Trials

One of the things God showed me was the caliber of woman I had found in my childhood sweetheart. Our daughter, Caprisha, was three years old when we decided to get married. Again, a very young couple, me with a disability, yet Cheryl was willing to marry me. Some folks actually said to her, "Are you sure you want to marry him? You know he is a sick man?" Her response was always, "I love him, and that is all that matters." Cheryl was shocked when on a shopping trip with a close friend, they were having lunch when her friend asked; "Cheryl, are you sure you want to marry James? After all, it's not going to get much better, and suppose you have more children, how will you manage if his health doesn't hold up?" Outdone, Cheryl responded emphatically. "I'm 100 percent sure our future will be what it will be; I trust God will be with us for all of it. That is how I am going to proceed." Cheryl's spirit would take us through many challenging times.

We struggled for sure, didn't have much, and were barely making ends meet, but we loved each other and worked very hard. Cheryl was working as a word processor. While I stayed at home with Caprisha, and continued to build things to help generate income. I remember being so broke one Christmas that we could barely afford to buy a $2.00 Christmas tree for Caprisha. But even so, we knew that things could have been much worse. We were just thankful that our rent was paid and we had food to eat. After only six months into our marriage, my kidneys failed due to Lupus, and I was placed on dialysis, a very stressful thing.

A catheter is inserted in your arm or chest and hooked up to a machine to cleanse your blood. Since you cannot urinate, the machine cleans out all the toxins from your body that urinating would. This procedure has to be done up to three times a week for at least 3-4 hours. After you're off the machine, you are exhausted and drained. It is also tough to take trips and go on vacations because you always have to be back for your treatments. You can set up the treatments wherever you go on vacation, but it takes the fun out of your trip. It is also imperative not to miss your treatments. In addition to all of this, the dialysis center was a very depressing place for me, and it wore me down. I could not see myself living like this for the rest of my life.

Dialysis happens when your kidneys are not adequately removing wastes and extra fluid from your body. Without urination, fluid builds up in the body and can cause swelling and shortness of breath, among other things. One day during dialysis, I experienced the urge to urinate—I felt a surge of hope—especially when it happened several times. I immediately notified the nurse, who called my doctor. He came in and ran several tests and came back smiling after he received the results. He shared with me that my kidneys had begun to function on their own again after only six weeks of treatments. The dialysis unit cheered for me, and Cheryl and I were thrilled. Finally, my doctor took me off of dialysis, and my kidneys would continue to function for many years.

It was a significant breakthrough regarding my health; God began to move in our lives in a mighty way. He just kept showing up because while I was yet on disability, we purchased our first home in 1984. We were so excited to become homeowners at such a young age, as had several of our friends. Buying this house was a total faith move. The house was not in the best of shape to the naked eye. Folks advised us that this was NOT the house because clearly, there was too much work to be done. Even our realtor had misgivings about us moving forward with the purchase, but we were determined. I put my skills to the test, and Cheryl's decorating skills came in handy as well. I actually looked at making this house livable for us in the practical application of all the research I had been doing on home improvement.

We discussed it, and I shared my theory with Cheryl; "Honey, it is one thing to read and study and research, but finally, you have to put the information you've acquired to the test—you gotta go get it done." And that is just what we did. I installed new cabinets, put in tile and countertops, and learned electrical and plumbing—which was new to me. There was a crawl space underneath the house, and I took on the task of installing cable under the house—which required me to crawl under there to complete. Although we were discouraged from purchasing this house, it became the ultimate showplace.

Cheryl and I were proud of what we had accomplished. And it didn't hurt that we loved to entertain and have family and friends over all the time. I fine-tuned my skills during this time, and I got better at building furniture and cabinets, and I received more calls to build for others. So, it was safe to say things were starting to look pretty good for us.

3

I Can Work Again

After being off work for a few years, I decided I was ready to go back and give it another try. I hadn't had any hospitalizations for a while, and overall, I was feeling much better. I decided to apply at the United States Postal Service. Even though I doubted they would hire me because of my health history, I made sure I was open about my health. During the interview process, I shared about having Lupus, having frequent hospitalizations, and the whole gamut. A few weeks later, I was called in for an interview after passing the written exam. I proceeded to get my doctor's ok and was hired as a mail carrier.

Even though I was now working a full-time job, I continued to build cabinets and furniture. By now, it had become my passion. It was soothing and allowed me to create for people, and I got a great deal of satisfaction out of that. In addition, given the fact that I had been stricken by a life-changing condition that I would have forever, being able to work with wood helped me to gain a sense of control; it was the one thing I could do that even the barriers that came with Lupus could not stop. I thoroughly enjoyed my work at the post office. It allowed me to meet and interact with all kinds of new people, and I could even secure new customers for my business. People were amazed when they saw the level of my cabinet-making skills. Yes, this work turned out to be very rewarding. Unfortunately, this joy was about to be drastically disrupted.

While working at the post office for only a year, a sharp pain shot up my left thigh as I was stepping out of the jeep to deliver mail. I tried to press through, but unfortunately, the pain got worse, and I could not continue to work; as a result, I was placed on light duty. I was hesitant to seek medical care because I was so concerned about losing my job. But of course, I couldn't keep putting it off (the pain was getting worse). Finally, the doctor referred me to a hip surgeon at UCLA Medical Center in Los Angeles. He advised me that my left hip had deteriorated because of the medication I was taking to help fight and control the Lupus—a steroid called Prednisone which was very powerful. I learned that I needed a total hip replacement as soon as possible.

My future at the postal service was unknown, and I became very concerned about my job. Cheryl and my father-in-law banked blood for my procedure in preparation for my surgery. Thank God it was successful. God continued to show His Presence despite everything. However, when I found out I could no longer carry mail, I also learned that some at the post office didn't want me to return to work, but they failed because my shop steward fought for me, and a new position was created for me. I became a router, I sorted the mail and put it in sequence for mail carriers to deliver. I was uniquely qualified for that job because of my past experience with delivering to numerous neighborhoods. Additionally, I was able to keep benefits, which I still have to this day—30 years later.

I was thankful to have my job still. I understood how special it was that this new position was created for me, and I had a smooth transition into it. The Lupus was in remission, and God was definitely on my side. It was then that I realized when God has something in store for you, nobody can stop it no matter how hard they try.

4

Our Family Grows

Our second daughter, Tiffany Nicole, was born a few years later. We call her our miracle child because we prayed for another child for more than five years. Because of my health problems, it had been a challenge for Cheryl to conceive. We also had the best nurse ever, Nurse Kim, who was also our best friend and had been there for us through thick and thin. While Cheryl was in labor and almost ready to deliver, our daughter's heart stopped beating.

Cheryl had to put on an oxygen mask to supply oxygen to our baby to help her breathe. Also, during this time, Cheryl began to hemorrhage and started losing a lot of blood. We weren't aware of what was going on, and the doctors and nurses didn't want us to panic, so they didn't tell us at that time. We later found out from Nurse Kim, who also helped deliver our baby, that she was in distress and almost didn't make it. Needless to say, we were thankful that everything turned out just fine. Finally, after eight hours of labor, Cheryl delivered a beautiful, healthy baby girl on August 26, 1987.

Tiffany Nicole would come home to the first crib I had built. After a few years and things were still going well, we decided to have another baby. I was still working full time at the post office as a clerk and still building cabinets and furniture. This time my wife conceived very quickly and without any problems. Everything went well with this delivery, and my wife was in labor for only two hours. Our beautiful third daughter, Jasmine Marie, was born July 3, 1989. Now that we had a house full of girls, we were satisfied with the size of our family and decided no more children.

5

A Test of Faith

In 1990, I began facing health issues again. I was in and out of the hospital with infections and other problems related to Lupus. Of course, it made it very difficult for me to work, but I was determined to hang in there for as long as I could. During my annual checkup for my hip that year—the one I had replaced seven years prior—I needed a revision. Hip revision surgery is necessary when a new hip is damaged either by infection or through wear and tear. I had to have it because I was still young and active and had simply worn it out. The surgery was scheduled a month later in Santa Monica, California, at St. Johns Medical Center by the same surgeon who gave me the first hip replacement.

The Lupus flared up during this time, and the healing process took even longer than usual. After things weren't getting any better for me, my doctor and I decided it was best to go back on total disability again. So after seven years at the U. S. Postal Service, I decided to retire; this decision was not easy and initially caused me a great deal of frustration and depression about having to leave a job I really enjoyed, I had fought hard to keep, and that gave me a sense of control. But, on the other hand, it had been very empowering to me to know that I could hold a job like a regular man despite my illness.

As time passed after this revision surgery, and I had stepped away from the post office, I started to build furniture again after a few months of healing and recuperating. And since I was now at home, I became the primary stay-at-home parent taking care of my daughters throughout the day. I had to help get them ready in the mornings for school, which included doing their hair, taking them and picking them up from school, attending the parent-teacher conferences, cooking, cleaning, and grocery shopping.

At this time, the skills I had acquired while growing up with four sisters and no brothers kicked in. My mother taught me how to do many things that women usually do. When I would show up at the girl's schools for activities and meetings, the teachers and parents were surprised to see that it was me most of the time and not my wife. On the flip side of everything I was going through, I thoroughly enjoyed being there for my girls, and I know they enjoyed having me around as well—bonding with them in this way was the hidden blessing; God kept moving, bringing light when it looked like we were in a dark place.

Additionally I was a father-figure to many of their friends growing up without fathers in their lives. My father had always been in my life, and until I became acquainted with these youngsters who did not have that, I saw that I had taken a two-parent household for granted. Along with this, I gained a great deal of respect for parents who stay at home and take care of the kids. It's a lot of work and very challenging at times, but I wouldn't have changed it for the world.

6

The Unexpected

Eight years had passed since we had purchased our first home. My health was holding out well, and the cabinet work continued to be lucrative and kept me quite busy. Then, in 1991, our daughters, 12-year-old Caprisha, 4-year-old Tiffany, and 2-year-old Jasmine, were thriving well, and it appeared things were smoothing out for our family. Consequently, we decided that we were ready to move into a larger home and set about looking for a new house; we went through the process and found a great new home. Regrettably, we'd soon learn that our train was about to jump the track again.

Before we were about to move into our new home, Caprisha was diagnosed with scoliosis (curvature of the spine). The condition was discovered during a routine exam at her school. This development blindsided us—but we knew we had to make the right move. So we immediately got an appointment for her to see a specialist in Irvine, California. Because her spine was curved so much, she needed surgery immediately. The surgery was scheduled a month later at UC Irvine Medical Center. It was devastating to all of us, and our daughter was frightened. Unfortunately, to make matters worse, she had to have two surgeries within two weeks of each other. The first surgery was to remove one of her ribs and the second surgery was to place rods in her back to straighten it up.

During this time, our family was going through some complicated things. We were back and forth to the hospital with Caprisha while at the same time navigating through the home buying process, preparing for the physical move, and still dealing with the emotional issues surrounding our daughter's illness.

When the time came for our move, family and friends came through and helped us get it done in one weekend while Cheryl was still in Irvine with Caprisha. In the meantime, thankfully, her surgeries went well and, after a few weeks, Cheryl returned with her to our new home.

Though Caprisha was recovering well but in a great deal of pain. A special brace was made for Caprisha that she would have to sleep in. As God would have it, Caprisha managed to get through it, and after a few months of recuperation, she felt much better and was able to return to school. In the meantime, all of our family and friends loved our new home on Oakwood Drive. It was also where I would meet a lot of new clients.

After settling in and Caprisha was doing better, I was able to get back to building cabinets and furniture again. Our home was on a busy street, and people would stop by often. The house was very warm and inviting, and we always made everyone feel very comfortable. It was the home my girls remembered and had most of their childhood memories. We would stay in this home for 13 years.

7

A New Knee

In 1995, I began suffering from severe pain in my right knee. Again, the medicine I was taking for Lupus was causing deterioration in my knee joint. At first, we handled it by the doctor giving me a brace to wear, hoping this would help and keep me from having surgery.

For a while, it did help, and I was able to continue building cabinets in my garage and caring for my daughters by rolling around in a chair. It did not bother me because I was duty-bound to do whatever I had to do to stay working in the gift God had given me. *"Whatever it took"* was my mentality.

Unfortunately, the brace was no longer working a year later, and I needed a total knee replacement because things weren't getting better. Once again, it was a repeat of my previous situation; surgery at the same hospital in Santa Monica, California, and the same surgeon who had done my hip replacements. By this time, I was wringing my hands with the sheer aggravation of it all. I was starting to get very tired of everything I was going through. I couldn't believe this was happening to me again! It seemed like whenever I would take two steps forward, I would get pushed back ten more. Yet, with it all, God was faithful. Finally, I had another successful surgery and came home after only a week in the hospital.

I also had to go to physical therapy for a few months, which was very intense. When I woke up, a machine was waiting to bend my knee.

To get my knee back to a 90-degree angle, they used a bike whose seat would get lower and lower each time. The lower it goes, the more you bend; this can be excruciating. It was a challenge, but being a former athlete helped me "press" through. In addition, my former athleticism would be helpful in all of the surgeries I encountered, counting the five hip replacements and a new knee.

After things got better for me, I returned to building cabinets and furniture. While making cabinets one day in my garage, I accidentally shot myself in my left finger with my nail gun. A few days later, I developed a fever and started feeling bad. I was hospitalized with a bad infection from the accident. The blood work didn't look good, and the Lupus had become active as well. While in the hospital, my condition continued to decline. The infection had taken over my body, and I couldn't breathe on my own; I was put on life-support and was fighting for my life. I don't remember much, but Cheryl told me the doctors said they didn't know if I would make it. Things didn't look good for a few weeks. Cheryl was back and forth at the hospital while still working, taking care of the household and the girls. She was stressed and drained as usual but never complained. I was so thankful for my family and friends praying for us.

But God . . . He truly stepped in, and finally, things began to take a turn for good, and after a few weeks, I was able to breathe on my own, and I was taken off life-support. Unfortunately, the tip of my left finger had to be cut off due to the infection. Within a few days, I was finally able to come home and recuperate.

As we always tried to keep things as normal as possible for our girls, we encouraged Caprisha to run in a pageant called "Miss Fashionetta," however the pageant occurred during the time I was in the hospital fighting for my life. This program was important because it encouraged young ladies to be all they could be and allowed them the opportunity to earn a scholarship for college. Caprisha had worked very hard and was going to practice every week. At first, I wasn't even sure if I would be there to see her participate in this significant event. But thank God I made it, and like the rest of my family and friends, we were very excited for her. Because I was just released from the hospital and still very weak, I couldn't do the father and daughter dance. I was very disappointed but thankful that a good friend filled in for me. I was, however, able to escort her along with my wife down the runway. It was indeed a miracle because I had been on life support fighting for my life just weeks before the pageant.

While walking Caprisha down the runway, I received big applause and a standing ovation because people knew what I had been through. I was very touched, and it made me feel good to know that people loved and cared about me. Caprisha won "Miss Personality" and "Miss Congeniality." It was an excellent experience for her and a night we will never forget. We were very proud of her, and I was thankful to be alive to see it.

8

More Hills and Valleys

Just when I thought things were getting better, my second daughter, Tiffany, was also diagnosed with scoliosis at the age of 10 while being tested at school. Tiffany was referred to a specialist in town and had to wear a special custom brace. She wore the brace for a few months, but unfortunately, it wasn't successful, and Tiffany was scheduled for surgery. So once again, we found ourselves in the same situation as Caprisha.

This situation was difficult to wrap our heads around! I wanted to pinch myself and wake up from this terrible nightmare. It's one thing when you are going through something, but when it's your children, it takes the anxiety to a whole another level. The surgery was a few months later at the same hospital, UC Irvine Medical Center, and the same doctor Caprisha had. Tiffany was very frightened and cried all the way to the hospital. We prayed with her and assured her that everything would be ok. Even though our hearts were just as broken as hers, we knew we had to stay strong for her. It was another very stressful time in our lives. Fortunately, Tiffany would only have to have one surgery to correct her spine, it went well, and Tiffany was doing great.

After being in the hospital for a few weeks, she came home. Tiffany recuperated well and returned to school after a few months. We discovered opportunities to enhance our lives with everything we were experiencing and all that we had to handle. While I still enjoyed my passion for woodworking, Cheryl developed an interest in African Art. She found she had a passion for it, and it also provided a creative outlet for her. Cheryl eventually got her wholesale license and started her own business. She sold statues, pictures, and figurines. We had to travel back and forth to Los Angeles to purchase inventory and would make a day of it. I was also involved in the business and helped her while still building furniture. We also painted most of our statues and made our ceramics, which kept us very busy. It turned out to be an incredible new bonding opportunity for us, something beyond my illness; again, God's hand in keeping us rewarded despite all we had to go through as a married couple.

We would have parties and shows and sell our art at different events. We had so much fun and would allow the girls to help us at times. It had become a family business for us. We eventually opened up a store for a short time where we sold many of our products. We understood the marriage vows more with each passing year, thinking of the "For Better or Worse," we were operating in the "Better," and we were grateful. The following year was very busy for us because we had a lot going on. During this time, I had hospital stays due to Lupus, but I could still build cabinets when I felt up to it. Cheryl was still working full time and enjoying her new business, which had taken off very well.

It was also the same year that our first grandchild was born. Caprisha delivered a beautiful, healthy baby girl named Daijah on July 26, 1996, who also brought a lot of joy into everyone's lives. Unfortunately, it was also the year that I lost a lot of people that I loved. The first was one of my best friends from high school who passed away from colorectal cancer at 37. It was challenging for me because we had lost contact with each other for many years and had finally reconnected and were starting to get caught up on each other's lives and were hanging out again when he got the news that he was sick. Even though we didn't have much time together, I appreciated every minute that we did have. Six weeks later, I would lose my Great Aunt, an Uncle, and my Grandmother, all within six months of each other. They all meant a lot to me and played very important roles in my life. I couldn't believe all of this was happening at once!

While things were still going pretty good for me health-wise, Caprisha was preparing to get married. I felt pretty good and was determined to walk her down the aisle. The ceremony was extraordinary because her grandfather, my father-in-law, performed the ceremony. She was one of the prettiest brides I had ever seen. I was once again the proud father.

Within a few months, Caprisha moved her family to Atlanta, Georgia. We weren't too excited about it because of the distance, but we knew we had to let her "be an adult." Of course, we could not see her or my granddaughter much, but we made sure we always kept in touch. The times we were able to visit them were some of the happiest times in our lives. On occasion, they were able to come to visit us as well. Over the next eleven years, she would bless us with three more beautiful grandchildren while living in Atlanta.

A year later, I would have to have a 3rd revision in my hip, to my great dismay. Although it started just as before, I noticed more pain in my left hip, where I had the second revision eight years earlier. Thankfully, the surgery was victorious once again, and I was able to go home after a few weeks. During this time, I was given the nickname "The Bionic Man." My spirits were down, and once again, depression set in. I wanted to give up, but I began to think about my family and friends who had been by my side from day one. I knew they were praying for me and encouraging me to hang in there. I knew in my spirit that I had to keep fighting no matter how hard it got! I had to keep telling myself that giving up wasn't an option. After a few months of recovery, I continued my woodwork, which always made me feel much better.

9

A Time of Sorrow

My cabinet business was doing very well, and I hadn't been in the hospital for a few years now, which was a record for me. But again, misery and angst were awaiting us. One day while at home, I got dizzy and passed out. Cheryl had to call the ambulance for me, as she' did so many times. I became unconscious. While at the hospital, I was put on life support once again because I could not breathe on my own. It was then that I thought my life was over. I don't remember much, but I remember being very sad and thinking, "this is it." However, after being on life-support for more than a week, I could finally breathe on my own again. The doctor told me Lupus was active, and my blood pressure and potassium were too high, which caused me to pass out. Once again, I made it through and came home after a few weeks. I remember asking God once again, "Why am I going through this?"

My father-in-law was diagnosed with cancer and was fighting for his life during the same year. We had become the best of friends over the years, and I respected him. He was like a father to me, and I was like a son to him. He had become very mellow and humble during his latter years. He loved stopping by our house to visit and bring candy for his grandkids. He was always such a big strong man who never got sick. It was challenging to see him deteriorate right in front of us. He held on for as long as he could, and unfortunately, after six months of suffering, he passed away at his home. His death was very devastating to all of us and was very hard to accept.

Six months after my father-in-law passed away, my father became seriously ill. He had been complaining about pain in his hands and other parts of his body at times. When he finally decided to go to the doctor, he asked me to go with him. We had no idea we'd come away with the worse news ever and were utterly stunned when we learned that he had lung cancer and was given only a few weeks to live. I couldn't imagine what was going on that we were having such a barrage of pain and sorrow. Neither my father nor I took the news of his cancer very well, and now we had to go home and tell our family the bad news. My father was also my best friend and had always been there for me when I needed him. It was very devastating for my family and me. It was also difficult for me to visit him while he was sick. The man who was always there for my family and me was now leaving me. Before I knew it, hospice was called in, and my father passed away a few weeks later at home.

I was in shock and felt like I was in the middle of a bad dream. It all happened so fast! It was a lot to handle in such a short period—and I was still going through my health issues. I couldn't believe that the two most influential men in my life, whom I loved dearly and looked up to, passed away within six months of each other. Their deaths were going to take all of us a while to get through.

Wow, what a year.

10

Our Dream Home

As time went on, I got back into building cabinets and kept myself busy. And with God's help, Cheryl and I were able to move beyond the passing of our fathers. Blessedly, I was in pretty good health and hadn't been hospitalized for a few years.

In 2004, we decided to move into a larger home with a more oversized lot that would allow me to build a workshop for my cabinets. I had outgrown my 2-car garage and needed more room to do my building. Finally, we sold the house we lived in and called home for 13 years. We had to wait for our new home before moving in. A friend of mine, who is in the real estate business, knew our new home builder, and they were selling the house together. I took a chance and asked if I could build all the cabinets in our house, and yes, I could.

I was very excited and couldn't believe I would finally work in an actual workshop and not the garage anymore. We enjoyed going by and checking on our new home almost every week. It took four months, but finally, it was ready; and in January 2005, we moved into our new home. I was very proud of the kitchen and bathroom cabinets I had built. Everything looked great, and we were extremely excited. I continued to work in my garage until I built my workshop in the backyard. We loved our new home and continued to entertain and invite family and friends over all the time.

By this time, Caprisha was still in Atlanta and had four beautiful children, Tiffany was heading off to college in Atlanta, and my youngest daughter, Jasmine was a sophomore in high school. We were proud of this accomplishment; it was surreal considering my health issues and those negative experiences. But still, we strived to have a good life. Some said we were, trying to keep up with the Jones,' but nothing was further from the truth. Despite everything, we worked very hard, and God blessed us with nice things. We seemed to constantly explain ourselves for our blessings to those who couldn't understand that God was in the blessing business, even in the midst of our trials.

We knew in our hearts that we were not going to place material gain over God, and it was okay to have nice things as long as we didn't do that. And it was for that reason that we kept being blessed. Our fathers always told us that everyone isn't going to be happy for our well-being, and boy, were they right!

11

I Saw the Light

The following year started great for me. I hadn't been in the hospital for four years now. Cheryl decided to open up a Residential Care Facility for the elderly at our old house that we moved from. Fortunately, a friend of ours bought our old house, so we rented it for the business. I helped her out occasionally when I wasn't too busy with my own business. She was still working full time and had her hands full but was determined to make it work.

One day while at Cheryl's business, I got dizzy and fell to the ground, and began to have a seizure. My blood pressure and potassium were very high, which caused my heart to stop beating. Cheryl called 911, and before I knew it, the ambulance had arrived. I saw a very bright light as if I was on my way to Heaven. I remember walking towards that light, but it wasn't time for me to enter yet for some reason. I tried to go in but couldn't. It was like God was telling me I still had work to do here on earth, and he wasn't finished with me yet. Later, I was told that my heart stopped beating while in the ambulance on the way to the hospital. However, the paramedics restarted it again with their electrical shocks.

Once again, I found myself back in the hospital and on life-support. What man is on "life support" at least four times in his life? Thinking of that was genuinely unnerving. I was exhausted and ready to give up at this point in my life. I remember asking God, "Why am I still here?" And in that same instant, I thought of my wife, kids, and grandkids and knew that I had to keep fighting. I stayed in the hospital for a week, and though I pulled through once again, I'd been home only two weeks when the same incident happened again. My heart stopped beating, which caused my kidneys to fail. Again, I was back on life-support and fighting for my life. After coming out of the coma a week later, the doctor advised me that he'd have to put me back on dialysis—which I hadn't been on for 23 years.

This news was heartbreaking. I had to get prepared for the miserable consequences of dialysis. Three days a week, four hours each; aside from being physically draining, the entire process thrust me back into a severe state of depression. Most of the time, I could drive myself, and when I couldn't, Cheryl and our daughters would take me. The sadness and depression were consuming. I felt like I had no more life left inside me, and I told myself I couldn't go on like this. I remember talking to God and saying, "God, just take me!" And to top it off, I was getting a pacemaker.

However, although I was ready to give up, others wouldn't let me. In the meantime, Cheryl decided to close her business to take better care of me. She was so stressed trying to work, run her business, take care of the household, and take care of me. It was also starting to affect her physically and mentally, and she lost 40 lbs. within a few months. Tiffany, who was away in college, decided to move back home to finish college and help take care of me. I was truly thankful for a loving family that really cared about me. I knew then; I couldn't give up.

12

The Big Meeting

After being on dialysis for months and being told that my kidneys weren't getting any better, it was then I decided I didn't want to be on dialysis for the rest of my life. I couldn't even build cabinets because I would be so tired after my treatments. I was very weak and had lost a lot of weight. A few weeks later, I went to a meeting about having a kidney transplant and received information about the process.

When news got out that I needed a kidney donor to get off of dialysis, Several family members and friends offered to donate their kidneys to me. So it was yet another time, my family and friends let me know how much they loved me, and I was determined to keep fighting. Cheryl, of course, was the first to offer her kidney, but I decided I would rather have her help take care of me after the surgery. My four sisters then decided they would get tested for the transplant, and whoever was the best candidate would be the donor.

After several tests, the donor would be my younger sister, who lived in Northridge, California. We immediately began our testing at St. Vincent's Medical Center in Los Angeles, where the transplant would take place. We needed many tests, so we were back and forth in Los Angeles, and we both had to be in good health to do the transplant. I was very excited and couldn't wait for the transplant to happen. All I could think about was, finally, no more dialysis.

Unfortunately, the following year landed me in the hospital again. During the testing process for the transplant, the doctor saw something on my left kidney that looked abnormal. After a biopsy, the doctor told me I needed to have the kidney removed before the transplant. In October of 2007, the surgery took place. Later I found out that after removing my kidney, it was cancerous. I was living with only one kidney that wasn't functioning very well and needed the transplant as soon as possible because my life depended on it. After a few months of recuperation, I was given a surgery date for the transplant on January 16, 2008.

13

The Trials Continue— God Where Are You?

As I was getting mentally prepared for my transplant surgery, I noticed small sores on my legs, called lesions. The sores were excruciating and began to multiply. I went to a dermatologist and was diagnosed with an infection, which caused my body's lesions. The dermatologist treated me for a few months and then sent me to a wound care doctor when things weren't getting any better. As time passed, the pain became unbearable. The occurrence of this infection would post-pone the transplant for quite some time. My frustration and level of depression knew no bounds.

There seemed to be no end in sight. Then, one afternoon after coming home from a debilitating three hours at dialysis, I received a phone call that my mother was in a bad car accident and was at the hospital. My sister and I immediately went to the hospital, where we found our mother on life-support because she could not breathe on her own. It seems that my mother had a heart attack while driving, thus causing the car accident. Unfortunately, my mother did not make it. It was a most devastating blow to our family. The struggle was real for us now—multiple levels of struggles. Not only was I dealing with my mother's death and involved in the planning of her funeral, I still had to go to dialysis every week and deal with the painful lesions on my legs. By now, my health was sinking fast, and once again, I was ready to give up.

It was definitely the breaking point for me! After my mother's funeral, I became very angry at God, as I had never been before. I had so many questions to ask Him, and I wanted answers right then and there! The main one was, *Why Me?* I couldn't understand why I was going through all of this. I wanted to know what I did that was so bad that He would allow me to go through all of this. I began to analyze myself and concluded that I'm not perfect, but I am a decent guy that wouldn't hurt a flea. I've been a good father and a good husband, but most of all, I am a Child of the King! *God, Where Are You?* With the support and prayers from family and friends, I could finally make it through once again. I knew I had to stay prayerful and trust God in the midst of all of this. I just had to keep believing and trusting in His Word and believe that all of this would end real soon. I couldn't give up now, not after all I've been through. I kept telling myself; I know there is a light at the end of the tunnel.

A few months later, while at dialysis, I started experiencing sharp pains in my abdomen. I went to a specialist, and he discovered that I had an infection in my colon and needed to have emergency surgery right away. The specialist also told me that I would have to have a colostomy bag after the surgery for eight months until my colon healed. I had lost over fifty pounds by then, and the infections wouldn't stop coming. The lesions on my legs were deep and excruciating. My legs looked like a dog had taken big bites out of them. The pain was so intense that I would hold my legs and cry at times. Unfortunately, no pain medication or antibiotic was strong enough to relieve my discomfort or pain. I had to depend on God's Grace and Mercy to help me get through this. The colon surgery went well, and I was on my way back to recovery. I also had to carry around a wound-vac (for infections) that I had to take with me everywhere I went.

The colostomy bag was attached to my left side and was very embarrassing and uncomfortable. It also had to be emptied quite often. I was also told that I wouldn't have my kidney transplant until the infections and lesions were cleared up. Unfortunately, after only three months from my colon surgery, another infection was in my abdomen, and once again, I had to have emergency surgery to remove the infection. After the surgery, I stayed in the hospital for a few weeks before coming home. While still dealing with my mother's death and my health, I became very frustrated and depressed once again. It would also push my kidney transplant back even further. 2008 was one of the worse years of my life.

14

Hard to Say Good-bye

In the summer of 2008, I was still going through a lot but feeling a little better. Not only was I still dealing with some health issues, but we were also having financial issues since I wasn't able to work anymore. By this time, it had been over three years since I had built cabinets and furniture. On top of everything else, the economy wasn't doing very well, and we knew eventually we would have no other choice but to move out of our home to something more affordable. We had been there five years, and it was just starting to feel like home.

The thought of me leaving my workshop and the cabinets in my house that I built made me sick to my stomach. My wife was very encouraging and was looking forward to making a new start. I had to face reality and move on. Even though it hurt us both, we decided never to look back and concentrate on moving forward. We have never worshipped material things or put them before God. We also know that it's ok to have material things as long as you don't let them, have you!

With that being said, we knew what we needed to do, and we knew we would be back on our feet in no time. The main thing was getting me back healthy to have the transplant and start working again.

Before we moved, I decided to bring more joy into our lives. My wife's birthday was coming up, and the girls and I decided to give her a surprise birthday party. If anyone deserves it, it was definitely her. We decided it was also time to say "thank you" for all she's done throughout the years for our family. Nobody will ever know all the things she had done to keep our family together when I couldn't. Cheryl has made many sacrifices - taking care of the household, kids, working, going back and forth to the hospital, and taking care of me. And also, she had to be our children's mother and father at times.

Cheryl had many women tell her they don't think they could have done what she does. Her reply is, "I believe in my wedding vows, and I believe in God." Cheryl is such a strong woman. I know there were times when she was just as tired and frustrated as me, but she kept going on. When I am discouraged, she always says something positive to lift me up and encourages me to hang in there and not give up. I don't know what I would have done without her. We invited many family and close friends to the party. My sister took her shopping for the day and kept her out while the guests arrived at our house. We had the food catered from her favorite Mexican restaurant. The girls had done an excellent job decorating and getting everything together. Needless to say, Cheryl was shocked when she came home. Everyone yelled "surprise" when she opened the door. She cried and was very happy. It was another exciting day I will never forget.

15

Still Holding On

The year 2009 started with many challenges, but I finally got rid of the colostomy bag that I had been carrying around for almost a year. The surgeon reattached my colon, and I no longer had the humility of carrying around a colostomy bag.

For those of you who do not know, when you have a colostomy surgery, the surgeon will attach the end of your colon to the stoma (an opening in your abdomen wall that the surgeon makes for waste to leave your body.) The colostomy bag is a plastic bag attached to the stoma that usually hangs on the left side of your stomach to collect your feces waste since you cannot usually have a bowel movement. Sometimes, it's difficult for you to fit it properly, or if you have eaten certain foods that cause "gas," which may cause it to burst at any time or have eaten certain gassy foods and smells terrible. And it is always in the way and visible for everyone to see. Then, you have to change and clean it just like a baby's diaper. Anyway, thank God it was gone!

A few months later, more bad news came my way. Once again, my hip was worn out, and it was time for another hip revision. It would be my fourth hip revision in my left hip. All I could say at this time was, "Can I Please Get a Break?" The surgery was scheduled only a few months after having my colon reversed. Once again, I went to Santa Monica for my hip revision, which hopefully would be my last time. The surgery was successful, and I stayed in the hospital for five days. Unfortunately, the infections and lesions were still visible and active on my legs; therefore, I still couldn't have the transplant. I was very discouraged but did not give up hope. In the meantime, my sister and I could continue our testing for the transplant.

On a happier note, a few months later, our middle daughter, Tiffany, graduated from college and received her bachelor's degree in Psychology. We were all very excited, and it gave us all something positive to focus on. She had worked very hard and also helped take care of me. We invited family and friends over for a big graduation party. We were very proud of her. Also, a few months after Tiffany's graduation, Jasmine gave birth to a healthy baby boy named Jordan. We were so excited, and it had been years since we had a grandchild in the same town. He lifted my spirits and gave me another reason to keep fighting for my life. He came at a time when I literally told God, "I can't do this anymore," and had basically given up. Jordan would be our fifth grandchild.

16

I Still Believe In Miracles

At the end of 2009, we finally moved into another home that was more affordable for us, and we were hopeful that one day we would become homeowners again. At this time, our last two girls had all grown up and moved out of the house, so it was just Cheryl and me at home. We had never experienced this before, and it was bitter-sweet. We missed them, but it was also good knowing that they could make it independently. We felt that even though we had been through a lot, we were confident that we also did our best job as parents.

We are not perfect, and neither are they, but we taught them the importance of responsibility, and it gave us peace knowing they could make it on their own. We are very proud of all three of our daughters, who have blossomed into beautiful young ladies. My health was finally looking good for me. The infections and lesions on my legs had finally cleared up.

I was determined this would be my year for the kidney transplant. Even though my sister was a perfect match, we still had to go through many months and years of testing. It almost made me want to give up because it is so much to go through. Because of my history with Lupus, the doctors wanted to make sure my body was ready for the surgery. I had to remind myself that a kidney transplant is a significant surgery not only for me but also for my sister. Every time we got closer to the transplant, an infection or lesion would come on my body and delay the surgery. By this time, we had been waiting patiently for nearly two years for the transplant to take place.

Finally, every doctor gave me clearance for the surgery. All the infections had cleared up, and the Lupus was back in remission. All I could do was cry and thank God that the big day was finally coming. My surgery date was set for July 7, 2010. I couldn't believe that I would be a new man in a few weeks. My family and friends were so excited for me as well. I finally could see the light at the end of the tunnel. All I could think about was, "No More Dialysis!" I truly do believe in miracles!

It was only a few months away from Mother's Day, and this one was looking extraordinary. Caprisha, who was still living in Atlanta, and had been for the last 11 years, surprised everyone and showed up at our doorstep. Her best friend picked her up the night before from the airport. Cheryl immediately fell to the ground, and we both began to cry. It had been a few years since we had seen her and we were both so excited! We enjoyed visiting with her for a few days and didn't want her to leave. A few weeks later was also very exciting. Jasmine graduated from Junior College with a degree in Business and Communications. She had worked very hard and decided to stay in college even after her son was born. It gave us another joyous occasion to celebrate. We were very proud of her. By the time summer had come, we had found out that Caprisha would be moving back to Bakersfield right before my surgery with our four grandchildren. It made us all very excited, and I was even more eager to have the kidney transplant so I could spend more time with them. I always wished Caprisha and the grandchildren lived closer because we could only see them a few times a year due to the distance. So not only would I have a new and improved body very soon, but my grandchildren will be here to share it with me.

17

The Transplant

We met early that morning at St. Vincent's Hospital in Los Angeles, and everyone was feeling good and hopeful. I still couldn't believe the kidney transplant was about to take place, and I couldn't sleep the night before. I wanted to pinch myself and make sure I wasn't dreaming. My surgery prep room was right next to my sister's, making it really nice. We were able to communicate and see each other right before our surgeries. All the doctors and nurses were amazed that my sister was giving me a kidney, and of course, I was very thankful as well. She had surgery first with a smile on her face, and when her surgery was almost over, they brought me in. I was overwhelmed, excited, and nervous, all at the same time. The surgery took a few hours, and we both were fine with no complications.

I immediately began to urinate for the first time in four years on my own. I felt so energized and refreshed. Wow, what a miracle! I was doing very well and was able to go home after a week. I had a lot of medication to take every day, but I was used to it. My sister was doing very well, too, and was able to go home after a few days. She was back to work in no time. It felt so good to be at home in my bed again. Things were going quite well for me for the first few days, but I began to notice sores on both of my legs as time went on. The lesions had come back! I immediately said, "Oh no, this is not happening to me again." I had also noticed swelling in my feet and ankles which is a sign of rejection from my new kidney. I called my doctor and went to see him the following week. Unfortunately, the lesions had not cleared up before seeing the doctor, and I was immediately put back into the hospital. I was very disappointed and upset. I had to stay in the hospital for another eleven days until the infection cleared up. I was finally able to come home once again.

Once I got home, I was feeling pretty good. I had a lot of restrictions for the first six months and couldn't be around too many people because my immune system was low. My doctors were concerned about catching germs and getting more infections, affecting my kidneys. The few people around me had to wear a mask like mine to cover their mouth and nose. My grandchildren couldn't be around me much either, which made it very difficult for me, but as we all know, children are the primary carriers of germs. As time went on, I felt pretty good and started to get back to my normal self again. I started working on airplane and boat models to pass the time away. I enjoyed the holidays with family and friends, and things looked very positive for me. I was still going back and forth to Los Angeles often for my checkups, which always ended in an excellent report. I was still very bored but knew I had to be very careful. I was very anxious to get back to my woodwork, but I knew I had to take it slow.

18

Can I Get a Break?

After the holidays, I began to notice a sharp pain that would shoot up my left thigh. It was on the same side that I had just had a hip revision the year before. I immediately called my doctor and made an appointment to see him. He told me that another bone close to my hip and thigh had deteriorated because of my Lupus medication. He also said that the bone was loosening in my left thigh connected to my hip, and I needed another hip revision. I was then referred to a doctor at UCLA for an examination. I felt like somebody had just knocked me down, and I couldn't get back up. I couldn't believe this was happening to me again!. I hoped that everything else would be OK once I got the kidney transplant.

Once again, my spirits were down, and I was very depressed. Finally, after a few months of no improvement, the doctor said it would be necessary to have surgery to correct the problem. I couldn't believe that not even a year had passed since my transplant, and I had to have another surgery! All I could say was, "Can I get a break?" By this time, the thought of hospitals made me sick to my stomach. The surgery was set for June 15, 2011, which happens to be a few days after my birthday. My family wanted my birthday to be special because I was turning "50" years old. It was definitely not the kind of birthday I had in mind, but I was reminded to be thankful that I was still around. While I was waiting to have surgery in a few months, Jasmine asked me to make her a queen-size bed. She had been sleeping on a full-size that I had made for her when she was eleven.

I felt pretty good and thought it was good to start back building again. By this time, I hadn't touched or seen a piece of wood in over three years. I was very excited and figured this would be the best way to keep my mind occupied as well. It felt so good to be back in the garage building furniture again. It felt like old times. After working on my daughter's bed for a few weeks, I finally finished it. My daughter was very excited and loved it. Eventually, word got out that I was back building furniture and taking on a few more small jobs.

I knew I had to start back slowly and not overdo it. Cheryl, of course, made sure of that. A few weeks before my surgery, I felt down about having another surgery again. My spirits weren't the greatest, and once again, I found myself getting very depressed. However, Tiffany graduated with her master's degree, which lifted my spirits. I made sure the surgery was scheduled after this occasion because I didn't want to miss it. After the graduation ceremony, we celebrated with family and friends. We were very proud of her and sent her to New York for her graduation gift. It was one place she had always wanted to go, and I'm glad we were able to make that possible. It is another special day I will never forget, and it helped take my mind off of the surgery that I would have to face soon.

19

The Big Surprise!

My birthday was coming in less than a week now, and I was still trying to figure out what I wanted to do. I didn't want to make a big deal about it, but I knew Cheryl and the kids wanted to do something special. Little did I know, they decided to have a surprise 50th birthday party for me at the Four Points Sheraton Hotel. They had been planning it for months, right under my nose. Cheryl told me we were going to someone else's surprise birthday party on the day of the party, and I fell for it. As we walked into the hotel, to my surprise, there were about 65 people that yelled "surprise." I couldn't believe it! And I saw many people whom I hadn't seen in years. It was breathtaking. I felt so much love in that room.

We ate, danced, played games, there were even speakers who said really nice things about me. My daughters also put together a lovely slide show of old and recent pictures of me with family and friends. At the end of the slide show, my five grandchildren said extraordinary things about me. It was very touching and brought tears to my eyes. Also, at the end of the program, I was able to speak and thank everyone for coming and for helping. I was very choked up and was genuinely lost for words. I didn't want the night to end. It was definitely a memorable birthday that I will never forget and really appreciate. It also reminded me of how many people truly love me and are praying for me. I knew at this point that I must keep fighting and couldn't give up!

The day had finally come for my fifth hip revision. My surgery was scheduled for 4:00 pm. I was glad it wasn't an early surgery like usual, and we had plenty of time to get to Santa Monica. The traffic wasn't as bad as I thought it would be, and the weather was much cooler in Santa Monica than at home. Even though I wasn't looking forward to the surgery, it always made me feel so much better with Cheryl by my side.

Once we arrived at the hospital, everyone was friendly and helpful. After finishing all the paperwork, I went to the pre-op room, waiting to have my surgery. Before I knew it, I was wheeled into the surgery room. The doctors weren't sure if they would have to replace my whole hip or just a portion. It all depended on how it looked once they were inside. After my surgery, I was wheeled into the recovery room. Unfortunately, the doctors told me they had to replace my whole hip because there was too much damage. He told me that I had a total of fifty staples in my hip and thigh area, and the incision was twenty inches long.

The surgery took three hours. During surgery, I lost a lot of blood and had two blood transfusions. I was immediately given a total of four pints of blood. I stayed overnight in the recovery room because my heart rate was high, and my blood pressure was low due to the stress on my body from the surgery. The next day, I transferred to a regular room once my vital signs were back to normal. As usual, Cheryl requested a roll-away bed for her to sleep right next to me.

The physical therapist wasted no time getting me out of bed the next day. Finally, I could stroll very slowly with a walker. It was so painful and hard for me, but I was very determined. I knew I had a long road ahead of me, but it's nothing I wasn't used to and hadn't been through before. Our phones were ringing off the hook, and several text messages from family and friends were concerned about me.

To brighten up my day, my three daughters and grandson came to spend the day with me, which was Father's Day. I was pretty down about having to be in the hospital on that day, but it definitely lifted my spirits when I saw them. Finally, after six days in the hospital, I was doing much better and was told I could go home, but I would have physical therapy to help me walk and get my strength back. I couldn't wait to get in my bed, and neither could Cheryl.

20

No Place Like Home

I was very eager to get back home again. The ride home wasn't as bad as I thought it would be. It felt so good to be back in my environment. I always tell my wife, "There's no place like home." The first night was pretty good. I was so stiff and sore, but I felt more comfortable being back home. The following day I tried to move my leg and realized I couldn't and would need much help. It finally hit me again that it would take some time, and I couldn't rush it. I felt so lost and helpless. I immediately broke down in tears for the first time in front of Cheryl. And, as usual, she assured me that everything was going to be all right. I could see the tears in her eyes and the frustration on her face as well, but Cheryl knew she had to be strong for me. I knew I had a long road ahead of me that nobody but God could help me make it though.

The nurse and physical therapist wasted no time coming over to check on me the next day. They would be coming every week until I was strong enough to be on my own. Physical therapy was tough at first, but eventually, it got easier. I had a doctor's appointment to get my staples taken out in a few weeks, which I was not looking forward to. I was so glad Cheryl wasn't going back to work for three weeks. I always feel more at ease with her around. I had many family and friends come to pray with me and give me words of encouragement, which I needed very much. They also brought food so my wife wouldn't worry about cooking. I must say, this is the most challenging surgery and recovery I have ever had to go through, and I couldn't have done it without everyone's help. I was very thankful for having these special people in my life.

The day finally came, and I went to Santa Monica for my postop check-up. The ride on the way was very challenging. The freeway was rough and bumpy and did no justice for my hip. When we finally arrived, I was just thankful that we had safely made it there. We parked right next to the elevator, making it very convenient for me. Everyone was accommodating by holding the doors open for me and waiting very patiently for me as I walked very slowly with my walker. Even though I was very grateful, I felt very helpless and couldn't wait for my recovery to be over. The doctor gave me a good report and ended up only taking out half of my staples. He said he didn't want to take all of them out too fast and that my incision needed more time to heal. It was no fun as he began removing some of the staples, but I've been through more challenging times, and I've learned to grit my teeth and bear it. I was told I would have to come back in a few more weeks to get the rest of the staples taken out.

Thank God the ride home wasn't as bad as it was going, and I couldn't wait to get back home and relax after my check-up. It had been a very long day for both of us. A week later, I had a doctor's appointment with my doctor in town. Unfortunately, I could tell I wasn't recuperating as quickly as I should have been. Since I had lost so much blood during my surgery, my doctor said my blood count was still very low and he gave me a few more prescriptions and told me to take it easy. I had lost over ten pounds and still didn't have much appetite. I was just thankful that I wasn't put back in the hospital that day!

21

A New Man!

It was a few days before the Fourth of July, and I was so excited that my family was coming over for a big barbecue. My kids and grandkids always perk me up and make me feel better when they are around. We had a wonderful time together even though the weather was so hot. There was plenty of good food, and the kids played games and had so much fun. But all I could think about was the next day, which would be my wife's 50th birthday. I felt so bad that I wasn't physically able to do much for her birthday as she had done for mine. But, of course, she wasn't disappointed and was very understanding as usual. I'm glad she was able to enjoy a special lunch with our daughters and a special dinner with her friends. All I could think about was how fast I wanted to recuperate so I could make it up to her. As weeks passed by, I felt myself getting stronger.

I finally had the rest of my staples taken out and got around much better, and my doctor said I could put all of my weight on my hip. I started walking with crutches instead of the walker. And after a few weeks, I graduated with a cane. It felt so good to be getting back to normal. I started physical therapy outside my home and could even drive myself. The doctor ordered physical therapy for six weeks. It also felt good to be independent again. I don't like relying on others if I don't have to. Even though I'm thankful for the help, it hurts me to see my wife go to work ten hours a day and come home and wait on me hand and foot.

I went to my first outing at a restaurant for my granddaughter's 15th birthday dinner a few weeks later. I was a bit nervous about going at first, but I knew I would have plenty of help. I was getting around quite well on my crutches and had no problem by this time. It felt so good to get out of the house for something fun and exciting other than doctor appointments. We had a wonderful time and as usual, just being around my girls and grandchildren always makes me feel good.

A month later was my grandson's birthday party. I was very excited about going to his party because, on his last birthday, I had just had my kidney transplant and wasn't able to go. My grandson was turning two years old. It would be my second outing since surgery. I was getting stronger each day, and my appetite was also getting much better. Within a few weeks, I could walk entirely on my own, and with the help of God and physical therapy, I could feel myself getting back to normal. I couldn't wait for the day to come when I would be able to start building furniture again. That was still the one thing that kept my mind occupied and kept me busy. I thank God every day for the gift he has given me. I know now that He knew it would come in handy one day and that it would have a purpose in my life. I've never felt so good in my life!

My whole body felt so great since the transplant and hip replacement. I could really tell the difference. I felt like a new man, whole and complete once again. It's been years since I felt like that, and I am excited about it. I am so thankful for a second chance at life.

Meanwhile, Cheryl planned on retiring from her job after working thirty-two years for the County. I was so glad she had finally decided on a retirement date, November 3, 2011. If anybody deserved a break, it was her! I was looking forward to having her permanently at home and seeing her more often. Before Cheryl left work, her job gave her a very lovely retirement luncheon at the office, and the same weekend we had a retirement party at the house for her with our family and friends. She would now keep a closer eye on me and keep me in line, which I knew I needed.

Well, another year has come, and I was so thankful that I could see it and go into it healthy. 2012 would be another fascinating and busy year for our family. First, Tiffany got married, and I was proud to walk another daughter down the aisle. Later, that year she gave birth to our sixth grandchild, Aden. A few months later, Jasmine graduated from college and received her bachelor's degree in Computer Graphics. These were very emotional times for me because I was always unsure if I would even live to see any of my daughters grow up and become adults. I was also blessed to stay healthy throughout the year and start back building cabinets and furniture.

22

The Greatest Love of All

2013 was the year I had been praying and waiting for! Cheryl and I were coming up on our 30th Wedding Anniversary, and we had plans to renew our wedding vows. We were supposed to renew our wedding vows on our 25th Anniversary, but my health didn't allow that to happen. I couldn't wait to tell the woman of my dreams just how thankful I was to have her in my life and to let her know how much I really appreciate her love and dedication to me.

After months of preparation and planning, the day had finally come. Cheryl had everything in order, and everything looked so beautiful and perfect. She used her favorite color, purple, to decorate. Some of our family members and a few special friends were a part of our bridal party. We also had our best friend perform the ceremony. It was extraordinary for everyone because they knew what we had been through throughout the years. I was so excited to see so many people that came from far and near to share this special day with us. With about 100 people attending, we renewed our wedding vows and shared our love again in front of everyone. I began thinking back thirty years ago during the ceremony and became very emotional about what we both have been through. I was so thankful that I was still living to marry the love of my life once again. She looked even more beautiful than at our first wedding, and I loved her even more. She didn't have a clue of what she would be getting into thirty years ago, but she loved me enough to marry me anyway. She not only married me but stayed with me during my hard times. Wow, what more could I ask for!

During the ceremony, she surprised me and serenaded me with our favorite love song, "Inseparable" by Natalie Cole. There were also a few people there that were at our wedding the first time. Neither one of us wanted this night to end. It felt like we both had fallen in love all over again. The food was great, and we partied all night long and had a wonderful time. We would also become homeowners again and move into our new home a few months later. We were very excited and thankful to God for making that possible again. But most of all, it felt good to be alive and well again! God is Good!

23

Cheryl's Journey

When asked to write this chapter on what I had gone through with my husband, James, I became very emotional while looking back over 38 years of my life and reminded of what had taken place. It took a while for us both to write this book because it was so hard to relive the reality of the pain, challenges, and difficulties we both went through beginning at such an early age. I had no idea that the man I fell in love with and married would go through so much pain and suffering at such an early age.

Neither one of us had ever heard of the word Lupus and had no clue how it would affect our family and our lives. I've been asked many times, "Why did you marry a man that you knew was sick?" My answer is and will always be, "Because I truly love him." I really appreciated everyone's concern, even with a few people still trying to talk me out of marrying him and not agreeing with my decision. So many people have also told me they wouldn't have been able to stay in the marriage and handle what I went through. My response to them is, "Everyone isn't strong enough to handle it, but if you truly love someone and are serious about your wedding vows that you made before God, especially the part that says, In sickness and in health till death do us part," then you could at least give it a shot!" I don't believe any of us are thinking about sickness or death when we repeat our wedding vows. All we know is that we are so in love with each other and can't wait for the honeymoon. We truly believe that everything will be wonderful and we will live happily ever after. I often tell young ladies before they get married that it's not about the wedding, it's really about your wedding vows. We put so much emphasis on the wedding sometimes that we forget about the rest of our lives.

I encourage parents to sit down and talk to their children about what marriage is before they walk down the aisle. So many mothers want that dream wedding for their daughter because they couldn't have it. But after that glamorous wedding is over that you spent your last on, reality eventually sets in. I've seen so many couples spend thousands of dollars on a glamorous wedding and not stay married because they didn't realize and nobody bothered to tell them about the work it takes to stay married. Being married is a big commitment, and it's about compromise and communication, just to name a few. But, unfortunately, a lot of couples don't understand what they are getting themselves into until it's too late. Although we don't have the perfect marriage, I always knew in my heart that I would stick by my husband's side while he was going through this transition, and leaving him was never an option for me. I have always been a strong person. I have always handled stressful situations pretty well and remain calm. Even though I am fairly quiet, I am constantly thinking and observant. I can say that my actions definitely speak louder than my words. I finally concluded that this is how God made me, and He definitely knew what kind of person my husband would need in his life.

God knew even before we did the things we were going to face. He also knew that it had to be someone strong enough to handle it and wouldn't leave him when things got tough. I believe that I was created just for him. Being a strong person has its ups and downs and comes with a price. Because you are the strong one, people will lean and depend on you a lot which can sometimes put pressure on you. It also means for a season. And then there are those that he puts in your life forever that will see you through to the end no matter what. I am so thankful for the people who did encourage me and stood by my side no matter what. I am so grateful for their prayers and their shoulders to cry on when I was having a breakdown and couldn't even pray for myself. I have to admit that the things I have seen with my eyes are truly unbelievable and miraculous, and I know it was nobody but God who brought us through.

I also have no problem admitting that watching my husband go through all of this was not easy. There were times when he wasn't the only one asking God, "Why?" It was me as well. But I would be lying if I said there weren't times when I felt like giving up just like he did. There were times when I wanted to run away and come back when everything was under control.

There were even times when I fell to the ground and told God, "Ok, he's gone through enough!" And yes, there were even times when I said, "God, I can't take it anymore!" I even felt at one point that I was losing my mind while trying to take care of my husband, children, the household, working full time, and running a business. Even as strong as I was, it became difficult for me to be everything to everybody. During this time, I also accepted that I had to be a mother and a father, which was very challenging at times. I realized I had spent most of my time and life at hospitals and being my husband's caregiver. I also discovered all the things I had missed out on and what I had to give up to care for my husband and my family. But if I had to do it all over again, I would. Of course, I wished things could have been different for us, but I also knew we were going through this storm for a reason but only for a season.

Whenever my husband was in the hospital, I was always afraid of leaving him, especially when he was on life support--afraid that he wouldn't be alive when I got back, so I wanted to spend every minute with him. I always knew that I couldn't sleep if I went home because I was afraid of receiving a phone call that he didn't make it through the night.

But I also knew that I had three little girls at home that needed me as well. I didn't realize how big of a responsibility I carried on my shoulders for everyone, and sometimes it wasn't easy to balance. I can't begin to explain the pain you feel while your husband is lying in the hospital lifeless and death is staring you both in the face. So yes, fear set in at times, and a lot went through my mind whenever he was in the hospital.

A few times, the doctors told me to make arrangements because they didn't think he would make it. But there was one thing I knew that would hurt me the most, and that was, having to go home and tell my girls that their father would not be coming home ever again. It came close so many times, but I was determined that it wasn't going to happen. That's the one thing that made me stay on my knees and in my Word even when I didn't feel like it. I knew I had to constantly trust and believe God for his healing no matter how hard it was and what things looked like, regardless of what the doctors said. With tears running down my face and pain in my heart, I was so determined and had to believe that my husband would live and not die.

Unfortunately, after many years of distress for my family and me, it all finally caught up with me in 2006. It was one of the worse years for my husband's health. My husband was in the hospital on life support for the sixth time and had been in and out of the hospital at least 60 times; I had finally had enough. I became furious and frustrated more than I had ever been before. It was also during this time; I shut down from the world as things seemed to be getting worse for my husband. I went into a deep depression, lost over 40 pounds, and had no appetite.

I threw my hands up and said, "God, I can't do this anymore!" I felt like someone had sucked the life out of me. It was then that I understood; I was just tired, mentally and physically. I felt like I couldn't go on anymore and wanted to give up! I didn't like the person I had become, and my heart had become so hard, and I didn't want to be around anyone. I felt like a big part of me had died! Of course, I didn't expect anyone to understand what I was going through, and it wasn't personal, but if you haven't walked in my shoes, you really can't comprehend my mindset at that time.

Unfortunately, my mind, body, soul, and spirit had shut down, and I slipped into a very dark place. I wanted and only needed God at this point in my life, and I knew He was the only one who could bring me back to life again. I also realized that it was a wake-up call from God telling me to take care of CHERYL for once.

Because I had gotten so busy taking care of everyone else for so many years, I forgot all about myself. My platter was running over; I had gotten lost in the shuffle. As a result, my health and mental state began to suffer and fail for the first time in my life. While still working and taking care of my husband and family, I went into hibernation and didn't go anywhere but to work. Family and friends would still call and come by to check on us but had no idea of the mental pain and anguish I was going through. I managed to still keep a smile on my face and act like I was just fine like I had always done in the past. I remember looking in the mirror one day and telling myself, "Even strong people have a breaking point!" But as time went on, I was determined to get my breakthrough. I realized that I couldn't care for anyone else if I wasn't well myself. I was determined to take back what the devil stole from my family and me.

Eventually, through prayer and God's Word, I slowly got my appetite back and could eat again. God renewed my mind, and I felt better than I ever had before. I am thankful to God that I made it through my hard times. I tell people that I don't want an award or recognition for what I have done and will continue to do for my husband and family. I have been told that God will bless me, and He has greater rewards for me in Heaven. I believe I am already blessed to have my husband here with me, and I'm thankful by the grace of God, we have made it through some tough times.

I only did what a wife is supposed to do for her husband and family. I would never have thought I would spend 28 years of my marriage helping my husband fight through a life-threatening illness and multiple near-death experiences.

I would also like to encourage women going through similar situations with their mates to hang in there and keep trusting and believing in God. I know sometimes it looks hopeless, but don't give up. It is also essential to find someone you can talk to. Unfortunately, some people who started with you won't end with you. There will also be people that you feel will be right by your side through it all, but that's not always the case.

There were times when I would talk to people about my husband, and they would say, "He's still sick?" We both realized that my husband's sickness was an inconvenience to some people, or they felt like it was something that we were both doing wrong. But I had to learn to trust God and not put my trust and faith in people. But God always had the right people there for me at the right times. God always sends the faithful few to help see you through until the end. So you will definitely learn who will be there for you during the dark times. I've also learned the importance of taking time out for YOURSELF!

There's nothing wrong with grabbing some ME time, even if it's just a hot bubble bath with candles burning and listening to your favorite music, taking a girl's trip, or just having dinner with a friend. I had to learn the hard way that it's ok to step away from the hospital and get some rest or just take a break and let God replenish me. It doesn't mean that you are a bad wife because you're not there 24/7. On the contrary, this helps to keep your sanity. And last but not least, always remember, If I can make it through, so can you!

Conclusion

As you can see, life hasn't been very easy for me, but I am thankful to God that I am still here. It was tough at times for Cheryl and me to handle my health issues, but we also had to address personal issues that would arise as well. My greatest prayer every day is that I will continue to stay healthy and strong and enjoy life with my family and friends. I am so blessed that God has allowed me to take care of my wife and allow her to enjoy her full retirement that she worked so hard for and deserves. Even though I still have health issues that I am still battling at times, I am hopeful to continue to fight the good fight of faith. I have learned through all of this that it's the simple things in life that we take for granted. I've also learned to live each day to the fullest because tomorrow isn't promised to anyone. I also wanted to show and encourage people by what I've been through and to let them know how they too can come out on top. Finally, I am a faithful witness that the deepest level of worship is praising God despite the pain, thanking God during the trials, trusting Him when we're tempted to lose hope, and loving Him when He seems so distant and far away.

Unfortunately, while writing this book, Cheryl and Jasmine were diagnosed with Lupus in 2017. Jasmine suffered a stroke and had kidney failure, but we have already seen firsthand how God has kept her and is bringing her through as well. I will continue to believe that the same God that has kept me through all of this will keep them as well. We will always keep our faith and trust in God no matter what it looks like or what the doctors are saying, and we have also taught our children to do the same.

I love inspirational quotes, and I want to share a few with you:

> *At my lowest, God is my hope. At my darkest, God is my light. At my weakest, God is my strength. At my saddest, God is my comforter; You've only got three choices in life: Give up, give in, or give it all you've got. Your present situation is not your final destination; Hold on; pain ends, your setback is just a setup for your comeback; You may not end up where you thought you would be, but you will end up right where you need to be; God has a purpose for your pain, a reason for your struggles and a reward for your faithfulness, so Don't Give Up!*

And then there is the familiar saying,
PUSH-Pray Until Something Happens.

But the one quote I will never forget came from a person on one Christmas Day. I said,
"Merry Christmas, how are you?"

And his reply was,
"I'm fine; I have the greatest Christmas gift anyone can have. I have life, and you can't wrap that up and put it under the tree; it's a gift from God."

No matter what life throws at you, only you are responsible for what you do with it. Are you going to let it control you, or are you going to control your circumstances? As you can see, I have been in many situations when I thought the end was very near and thought my life would be over. But

God kept me here for a reason, for His purpose. God did not put us on this earth to be ordinary but to make a difference in this world and people's lives. I now cherish each day, but what seems more profound is the appreciation of a healthy life and taking nothing for granted. The experiences you endure in your journey through life will definitely alter the way you think. If it wasn't for God's grace and mercy and the support from family and friends, I wouldn't be here today.

I'm very thankful that I watched my little girls grow up and become very successful young ladies and walked all three of them down the aisle on their wedding days.

My life is a true testimony of what God can and will do if you put your total trust and faith in Him. I know it's not easy at times because we are human, and the devil is waiting for us to fail, but through prayer and God's Word, you can make it. So, for those of you who might be going through the same thing or similar, I would like to encourage you to hang in there no matter how tough it gets and never give up. If I can do it, so can you!

About the Author

James W. Nutt is a dedicated husband, father, and grandfather who resides in Bakersfield, California. He has been married to his high school sweetheart, Cheryl, for over 38 years. They have three daughters, Caprisha, Tiffany, and Jasmine, three sons-in-law, Darnell, Ivery, and Chris, and eight grandchildren, Daijah, Davione, Danaiya, Dillon, Jordan, Aden, Hailey, and Austin. James is a retired postal worker and an accomplished woodworker for over forty years. James is also a 40-year survivor of Lupus and a kidney transplant recipient. James is a walking miracle and has experienced the power and favor of God in his life.

The "Nutt" Family

Austin

Hailey

Information About Lupus

The disease can affect all ages but most commonly begins from 20–45 years of age. Lupus is more frequent in African Americans and people of Chinese and Japanese descent. It is also most common among women.

Resources:
Lupus Foundation of America, www.lupus.org
Lupus Research Alliance, www.lupusresearch.org
National Kidney Foundation, www.kidney.org

www.ingramcontent.com/pod-product-compliance
Lightning Source LLC
Chambersburg PA
CBHW060346130626
46553CB00003B/1110